Leading You Out of the Darkness Into the Light

~ A Blind Man's Inspirational Guide to Success ~

Maxwell Ivey Jr.

Leading You Out of the Darkness Into the Light:
A Blind Man's Inspirational Guide to Success

Copyright 2014 by Maxwell Ivey Jr.
All rights reserved.

ISBN-13: 978-1505867794
ISBN-10: 1505867797

No part of this book may be reproduced in any form or by any means electronically or otherwise, unless permission has been granted by the author, with the exception of brief excerpts for review purposes.

Cover image/photography: Copyrighted by Jenny Rollo.

Cover design: Angela from http://angelamccall.com/ (with permission from Jenny Rollo).

Cover modification and formatting for printing by Brenda from coversbydesign.net.

Layout, formatting, and editing by Lorraine Reguly of http://wordingwell.com/.

LEADING YOU OUT OF THE DARKNESS INTO THE LIGHT

Dedication

This book is dedicated to anyone who desires success.

Table of Contents

Contact Information 7

Introduction: Take My Hand 9

Step 1: Begin by Determining Your End Goal 15

Step 2: Assess the Situation 23

Step 3: Do What You Can, One Thing at a Time .. 27

Step 4: Take Action 33

Step 5: Ask for Help When You Need It 37

Step 6: Staying Motivated by Taking Small Steps 43

Step 7: Celebrate Your Accomplishments 49

Step 8: Find the Good in Everything and Be Positive 53

Step 9: Allow Positivity to Enter Your Life and Keep the Negativity Out 59

Step 10: Look at the Big Picture and Describe Your Success 67

Step 11: Assess Your Failures, Re-evaluate, and Repeat 71

Temporary Parting Words 79

About the Author 83

About *It's Not the Cookie, It's the Bag: An Easy-to-Follow Guide for Weight Loss Success* 85

About *The Blind Blogger's NYC Adventures (+ How You Can Make YOUR Dreams Come True)* 87

About The Blind Blogger's First Speaking and Signing Adventures (+ How You Can Conquer Your Fears) 89

LEADING YOU OUT OF THE DARKNESS INTO THE LIGHT

Contact Information

I don't want this book to be one that's filled with website links, and so I'm including this page here, with the bare minimum of information, so that you won't be distracted as you read through this book and complete the exercises I have for you as I guide you out of your darkness and into the light.

In some of the exercises, I ask you to email me. I'd like for you to use the email address justask@theblindblogger.net when you do. By participating in the exercises and emailing me, you are proving that you are accountable for your actions. This accountability will assist you as you take concrete steps towards achieving your dreams.

I have two websites: The Midway Marketplace (at midwaymarketplace.com) and The Blind Blogger (theblindblogger.net).

I've appeared on many websites as either a guest, as part of a podcast, or an interview. For more information, please visit my websites. I'd also like to invite you to become a subscriber so that you can receive special coaching offers and be informed before anyone else is. Simply visit The Blind Blogger website and sign up!

Introduction: Take My Hand

Hello. Let's shake hands. I'm pleased to meet you.

If you are reading this, then there is something in your life you want to accomplish. You either don't know where to start, or you have started already, but are stuck, and don't know where to go, or what to do next.

That's okay. With my guidance, I'll lead you out of your darkness and into the light, and I'll do it without making any jokes about "the blind leading the blind," too.

I didn't say that to be comical. (Okay, I did, sort of.) I said that because I'm literally a blind man.

Yes, I'm blind, but I run two businesses and have two blogs. I am rapidly becoming a well-known blogger, too, thanks to my honest and open style of writing and my positive, upbeat philosophy.

Did I get to this point alone? NO; no one does anything big by themselves.

Was it easy? NO; most things worth doing will take a lot of hard work, but I have done it.

Now I want to help you do it, too.

I want to help you overlook the excuses and overcome the obstacles. You have it all inside you, you just need a little help!

I'll give you a formal introduction now: My name is Maxwell Ivey, but all my friends call me Max, and that is what I hope we will become by the end of this book.

I want to become that trusted friend who you know you can turn to at any time, who will tell you what you need to hear, and who will tell you the unvarnished truth, whether you want to hear it or not. While you sometimes might not want to hear what I have to say, you should know I only have your best interests in mind!

I know I can help you because I will be sharing the exact methods—in the form of steps—that have worked for me. I will also relate some of my own experiences to you as we walk down your path together. Interspersed with these experiences will be exercises for you to complete, questions for you to consider, and goals for you to contemplate.

Throughout it all, I will be with you, guiding you out of your darkness, into the light.

To begin our journey together, I will share a few things about me, both general and personal. I will be completely honest with you, always. I have nothing to hide, and tell it like it is.

I am an almost totally blind gentleman from Conroe, Texas, which is near Houston, in the United States of America. I'm currently 48, and I run a business where I help people sell amusement equipment and related items, mostly online, but I want to travel more and have plans to start a YouTube video show where I will visit certain clients of mine on location. I am 6'4", weigh 250 pounds, and am in the best physical health of my life. I am a successful blogger and have also done many Google Hangouts. I have a wealth of supportive friends both online and off.

However, it wasn't always this way.

After the early death of my father ten years ago, my brothers and I were unable to keep the family-owned business going. We had operated a traveling carnival, like many of our relatives had done—and were still doing. After we went out of business, we had to go to work with my uncle's carnival. We had competed with his family for bookings, so this made the feeling of failure that much worse.

My health declined and I was on my way to an early death. I had high blood pressure, took a variety of medications, was morbidly obese, was depressed, and was not sure where I was going in life. I barely had the energy or passion to do much more than get out of bed each morning. I was sleeping on the floor of a travel trailer at the time, so even that wasn't much of a daily accomplishment.

Basically, I was a mess.

I started my transformation by getting healthy.

I found a good, primary care physician who convinced me to be tested for sleep apnea. The sleep study determined that I did indeed suffer from the disease. I was told it was severe and probably dated back to when I was a teenager. After being fitted with a CPAP (a breathing machine), I started to regain my energy and passion. I knew there was "something" better out there for me, but I didn't know what it was yet. The good thing was that I finally had my spark back. I had the desire to find out what that "something" was. I'm hoping that by seeing how I went about this, that you, too, can finally make that leap forward. I want you to feel the same feeling of success and hope that I feel each day when I arise.

Yes, I greet the day with anticipation. I don't know what it will bring. It won't always be good news, but it will be exciting, challenging, and make me feel like I am really doing something. Today, it's writing this book, which I never figured I would be doing. I never saw myself as an inspiration; I only saw myself as a guy who was working hard to make a living for his family.

Yes, I am blind, but I didn't see that as any big deal. I have been blind most of my life. It may be part of who I am, but it's not something I think about much, unless it gets in the way of what I am trying to do in the moment.

I'm sure you have your own struggles. You might have a nine-to-five job that isn't really nine-to-five any more. You might take work home and do work on your smart phones while commuting. You might be married, or in some type of relationship. You might be a parent or step-parent. You might be the caregiver in your family. You might not have a lot of education or formal training. You might come from a home where you were taught you would never amount to anything. You might have been abused in other ways. Whatever your struggles are, I know you have some, if not many. We all do; you are not alone.

For some reason, my being blind and running an online business has a way of motivating people to do more than they thought they could. If that is what it takes to get you to follow my lead and take action towards becoming that better self that you were meant to be, then I will be happy to be your inspiration. I would love to be your coach, mentor, role model, or whatever you want to call me.

If you are ready to *finally* accomplish those dreams of yours, then let's get started.

Step 1: Begin by Determining Your End Goal

Most of what I will share will revolve around starting a business or making your existing one grow; but the principles can be applied to anything you want to accomplish. Whether you want to quit your job, get healthy, learn an instrument, get a new degree, or raise money for your favorite charity, the path is the same.

Where do you begin?

Believe it or not, determining this is the hardest part. This is the place where you have to have the courage to be completely, brutally honest with yourself.

You have to open your heart and ask yourself, "What is it that I really want?"

I'm not asking you to say what you are supposed to want, or what your neighbor wants for you, nor do I mean what your parents taught you to want. I don't even mean what you feel like you can accomplish.

Instead, I want to know that one thing that *only you* know about—that dream that lives so deep down inside of you that you don't even whisper it to yourself.

Maybe you don't quite know what it is yet.

That's okay, too, and may be why you are here, seeking guidance from me.

Be assured, you've come to the right place.

I'm going to share some of my own decisions in this area and then I will have an exercise for you.

I started out wanting to be a carnival owner like my dad was, but my dad convinced me that, because of my blindness, I could help the family more by going to college and becoming a lawyer. I did my best to fulfill this goal, but I wasn't able to manage the law school admissions test.

I didn't want to admit failure, so I attended a training program where blind people were prepared to go to work for the IRS (the Internal Revenue Service). I convinced myself I wanted this, but it was not for me.

After two years of taking calls from people who were stressed by the possibility of government punishment for not filing their returns or not paying their taxes, I quit and went back to work for the family business. I did bookings, and I owned two games for children—a duck pond and a balloon dart. (I'm sure you've seen and/or played those games at fairs or amusement parks, as a child!)

My family was broke a lot of the time, but I was happy. I felt like we were building something, and I felt like I was an important part of the family's growth. While our carnival business was going downhill, I thought I had better start doing something else, so I began helping other people sell their equipment. I had helped my family when they needed to buy, sell, or trade rides; so I thought it would be a natural progression. I knew it wouldn't be easy, but I believed it was my best option.

I soon found out though that there was a lot of things I would have to learn.

I began with a website.

My brother, Michael, built my first website. Since then, I have had to learn how to hand-code a website using html, how to start a blog, how to build a social media network, how to run a WordPress-based site, how to record a YouTube video, how to run a Google Hangout, how to create a mailing list, and much more. I'm not mentioning this to brag, but as a way of showing you how little I knew in the beginning and how far I have come since 2008. Did I do it overnight? Obviously not. It's nearly the end of 2014 now.

Did I always know what I was doing? Heck, no. Did I do it all myself? Nope, I had help, but I did it!

Can you do the same thing? Yes, without a doubt!

I know you can, and I'm going to share with you exactly what I did and how I did it, so that you can learn from me and my experiences.

The most important step was the decision to take action and actually do something about my situation.

After I started to get healthy, I took some time to myself and studied my situation honestly.

I knew I wasn't going to be happy working with my uncle's carnival, even if my one remaining game could have made money on his midway. I didn't have the funds to invest in a different game or attraction. I didn't have a lot of skills (or at least I didn't think so at the time). I knew a lot about the amusement business and thought I could use the sales skills I had employed in booking our carnival to build a business as an amusement equipment reseller or broker.

I then thought about how to get started. I knew I would need a website and a domain name, but I didn't know anything about where to go from there.

After asking for help, Michael was able to find some tutorials online and got the site started. I knew I would still have to get clients, find buyers, post listings, set fees, collect commissions, etcetera. Even now, every day is a learning experience of some kind, but I am happy with the way my life is progressing.

You will be, too, if you put forth an honest effort.

Exercise 1

This exercise is not going to be physically hard, but it will challenge you. It also consists of three parts, so make sure you do each one.

Also, it's important to note that I will specifically indicate to you when you are to stop reading to complete the exercises; I'll do this at the end of each section.

Take at least fifteen minutes to yourself—with absolutely no interruptions—and write down what that one thing you really want for yourself.

Don't write down the superficial answer; I don't want the effects of being successful at your goal, like having a big house or fancy car, or being able to quit your job and spend more time with your family and/or take lavish vacations. Instead, I want you to find what it is that will make you the happiest person you can possibly be.

After you write down this main goal, write down one single, concrete action you can take today that will help to make it a reality.

Once you have this step defined, I want you to email me with your answers and some sort of proof that you have actually taken that first step. I don't just want to advise you—I want to be part of your success. The email address I want you to use is justask@theblindblogger.net.

It's okay if you take more than fifteen minutes, or even more than an hour, to complete this exercise. You might have to find this quiet place several times, but I promise you that the time you spend in reflection is very important. It doesn't have to be sitting still, but it does have to be free of distractions from family, television, smart phones, the computer, the Internet, etcetera. It can take place in the shower or while you are running. It can be as you sit quietly petting your dog or cat.

The point is to get you thinking about that one thing that you want badly enough to sacrifice for. It will be the thing that gets you out of bed early or keeps you awake at night. It will be the thing that just thinking about refreshes you and gives you energy. It will be that thing you smile about, laugh about, or cry over. It may also be that thing your friends and family don't understand. It might be something that your closest friends ask, "Are you crazy?" when they hear about it.

LEADING YOU OUT OF THE DARKNESS INTO THE LIGHT

If you take the time to really discover what it is inside you, the pure joy you will feel for even attempting it will make all of this worthwhile.

You may come up with more than one big idea. If this is the case, then you need to decide upon one of them to go after at this moment. I don't believe there will be more than one, but if there is, then choose the one that speaks to you more than the others do. It may be that the others will be natural progressions, stemming from your main idea or goal.

You will probably come up with many steps that you could take to accomplish your primary goal. If you do, then—by all means—write them down, too! *For now, the assignment is to pick just one and actually do something about it today.*

You can give yourself bonus points if, after taking this first step, you decide to share with more than one friend, more than five friends, or with a social media network. You may not want to tell everyone right away, but you need to celebrate this action by telling someone, which is why I want you to email me.

Stop reading now and complete this exercise. Once you have done that, come back, and continue reading. There will be another exercise for you soon! In fact, there will be one at the end of each step.

MAXWELL IVEY JR.

Step 2: Assess the Situation

You know about my starting the Midway Marketplace already, so I will share how I decided to start a second business as a coach, mentor, and public speaker.

I had been blogging for a while to promote my amusement equipment sales business. I joined several groups on LinkedIn and Facebook where you share your blog posts and comment on each other's work.

People started reading my posts and comments, and they realized I was doing this as a blind computer user. Many started commenting on how impressed they were with my writing. Others started calling me an inspiration. I began to get emails from friends, encouraging me to step outside my comfort zone and help more people by coaching and motivating them.

As I am told so often, if I can do this, what excuse does anyone else have? I finally accepted that, just by showing up every day and doing what I do, I inspire others. Once I accepted this, I took action.

I started a new blog, and wrote some posts for it. The response was so good, that I filed for a domain name and transferred my site from Blogger to WordPress. I did this pretty much on my own and with such success that even more people told me how inspired they were.

Next, I decided to create a coaching page. I was then asked to be a participant in an online summit and asked to write a book. The summit offer has since fallen through, but I chose to move forward with the book, and the fact that you are reading this proves that I finished it!

I also now have a legitimate email auto responder via Aweber. I didn't go looking for this, but once it found me, I took action.

To this day, I continue to grow in new ways on a daily basis, but taking that first step was very important.

It took courage to dig down deep inside myself, and it'll take courage for you to dig down deep inside yourself and find what you want out of your life.

t will also take determination and perseverance to continue down the path until you have reached your goal. At this point, the problem is information, technology, emotional overload, or a combination of all three. The Internet, libraries, friends and family often can provide a wealth of information on any topic, and the main problem for many people is there is ***too much information***.

I'm going to show you how I manage to avoid overwhelming or scaring myself, because it will help you with your journey.

First, I want you to do another exercise. This one will should be fairly easy, and you should be able to accomplish it rather quickly.

Exercise 2

Make a list of the things you would need to do in order to make your dream a reality. If you already started doing this, that's great!

Stop reading now and complete this exercise. Once you have done that, come back, and continue reading.

MAXWELL IVEY JR.

Step 3: Do What You Can, One Thing at a Time

I'm going to bet you that you probably put some things on your list that you wonder how you will ever manage. I believe I am right about this because this held true when it came to my own plans!

When I started, I knew I needed a website, but I didn't have the first clue how I was going to create one, and when I was told that I would need to have an e-book, I thought, "I don't know the first thing about writing an e-book or book, publishing one, or giving one away." Yet here I am, giving it my best effort!

In my attempts to understand the process, I began reading and talking to people. I learned some of the things involved in both the writing and publishing processes. When I encountered obstacles, I found ways to overcome them. I also started telling others what I was doing.

I even gave myself a few deadlines, and tried meeting them. When I missed one of my set deadlines, I didn't get down on myself; I simply set a new, more realistic one, as I realized that I was being overly optimistic! I have never written a book before, so this whole experience has been a learning process I embraced.

I hope you will follow this example and not let your fear about *the how* keep you from taking further action. There are *always* going to be skills, talents, and resources that you lack. There *are* going to be things you can't do today that you will be able to manage in a few weeks, months, or years depending on the size of your goal. And I can promise you *there will* be things on your list that scare you or at least cause you some level of discomfort.

I speak from experience when I say this, too. A good example of me stepping out of my comfort zone is the instance where I had to move a blog from one site to another, with no one to help me.

When I first started my site, The Blind Blogger, it was a free blog on the Blogger platform. I wanted to test out that platform; my experience up to that point was with WordPress.

After having that blog for a couple of months, I made two decisions: to move it to WordPress and to become self-hosted. I was worried that I would somehow break my site, lose my existing posts and comments, and look like a total idiot.

What made things uncomfortable for me was that the people I knew and trusted who could do it for me were otherwise occupied. *Not* doing it would have been an easy cop-out, but I had made a decision, and I wanted to stick to it—come hell or high water!

Basically, I had to face my fears and do my best.

So will you.

The good news is that it all worked out in the end. I made one minor mistake, but a friend who is a webmaster was able to find the time to help finish the move.

The truth is, if you picked the right goal, it should make you equal parts excited and nauseous!

I've been blogging for almost seven years now, and there are *still* things that I am learning.

I'm actually convinced that if you are living life the way it is meant to be lived, you will always find new challenges and new things to learn.

The point is: Do what you can *today*. Focus on one thing at a time.

If you can't do it now, then maybe you can learn to do it soon. If you can't learn to do it, then maybe you know someone who would be willing to do it for you. (This has to do with the idea of asking for help, which I will cover later.)

I want you to focus on one item to help you avoid the feeling of hopelessness.

I don't want you to ask yourself, "If I can't do it all, then why do anything?"

Too many people get caught up in waiting until they can do something perfectly rather than just doing what they can today and doing more tomorrow.

I may have an advantage here because I am blind; I have often had to put off things due to a lack of technical knowledge, proper tools, or the availability of someone to assist with a given task. Yet, if I waited for everything to be perfect, I would have never done anything at all.

I'd still be waiting to start my own business. Instead, I am now a recognized expert in the area of brokering amusement equipment and related items. I also have clients all over the world.

Now, I want to help you take action, so I have another exercise for you.

Exercise 3

Get a large piece of paper, and write your goal statement at the top. Once you have done that, I then want you to divide the paper into four sections, however you like. You could use columns or have four equal rectangles. Be creative!

Once you have it divided, label each section using the following headings:
I have it, I can learn it, I need help with it, and I can't do this right now.

Using the list you created in Exercise 2, I want you to recopy your list putting each item in one of these categories. If you have since thought about additional actions, then, by all means, add them to the list.

Be honest with yourself. If you have asked a partner or your spouse to be part of your goal, then they can help you evaluate your decisions about what needs to be done and what category to put each item in.

This is an important exercise; it will make things much easier for you later!

Stop reading now and complete this exercise. Once you have done that, come back, and continue reading.

MAXWELL IVEY JR.

Step 4: Take Action

Use your divided paper from Exercise 3 to get you started.

If you have the skill or resource, then I would like you to take action on whatever you can ***immediately***. Don't give yourself time to lose momentum!

If it's something you can learn, then you need to make arrangements to learn it, such as signing up for the training, for example, or finding tutorials you can use to teach yourself.

If it's something that you need to ask for help with, then make an appointment to approach the person you need to ask. If you don't know who to ask, post a question on Facebook that says something like, "Do you know who I can ask for help with (insert your problem here)?" You can post the same thing on Twitter, Google+, or elsewhere. Someone is bound to help you!

And if it's something you can't do now, then **put it out of your mind**. I know this is harder than it sounds, and I wouldn't be a bit surprised if you are sitting there right now thinking, "Max is nuts!"

If you take immediate action regarding the things you *can* influence, you won't have a lot of time for worrying about the few items *that are totally outside your control.*

This is basically my version of the Serenity Prayer as it applies to business. I do what I can, I don't worry about what I can't, and I ask God to show me the difference. (You can replace God with the universe, your higher power, or the deity of your choice.)

The point is that you want to be moving forward.

You don't want to be distracted or even depressed by what you *can't* do. If you continue to learn and grow, many of these items will be moved out of that category!

My goal is to help you accomplish your dream, and this technique works for me.

When I started, I knew I could recruit clients. I had done a lot of cold-calling and emailing to book events for the family carnival. I also knew a lot about the carnival and party rental segments of the amusement industry. I knew that I could learn to run a business. I knew I could learn to set my fees.

I knew I could learn about all the other areas of the industry such as amusement parks, water parks, circuses, etcetera, and I thought I could learn how to write ad copy for my listings.

I didn't know anything about building a website. It turned out my brother, Michael, did.

Before he made my first site, I had mentioned to a friend that I didn't have one. She volunteered to put a page up for me on her site. She even posted the images for me.

I can't edit or even select photos and videos, but my other brother, Patrick, could—and still does.

I had no idea about having a blog, recording podcasts, doing YouTube videos. I now do all of these.

I still haven't managed the logistics of doing videos on location with my clients, but I have gotten around this by having them send in videos that I incorporate into my own shows.

This is why I always tell people, "Do what you can, and do it *now*."

If you wait until tomorrow, you will never do it. There will always be a reason that keeps you from accomplishing your goal or living your dream.

Exercise 4

Take some type of action to move yourself forward, toward your goal. Only you know what that action is, or could possibly be.

Stop reading now and complete this exercise. Once you have done that, come back, and continue reading.

Step 5: Ask for Help When You Need It

I mentioned earlier that I was going to cover the subject of asking for help, and I am, now.

This idea probably won't bother you as much if your goal is to lose weight and get healthy, put in a garden, or learn to play a musical instrument, but it does seem to bother people running a business.

For some reason, people think asking for help is a sign of weakness. They think that potential clients or customers would be turned off if they found out you weren't Superman or Wonder Woman and couldn't do it all by yourself. They think that asking friends and family for help is a recipe for disaster. And even in this age of the Internet and social media, they fear opening themselves up online, fearing ridicule for not knowing something.

The truth is: We *all* need help.

Some people get this help by hiring consultants, paying for training courses, or buying into existing businesses.

Others—like me—do it by asking questions, reading blogs, joining groups, and approaching mentors.

I know that, when it comes to my own business, I would have made very little progress if I didn't get help from others.

As I mentioned earlier, my experiences might have been made easier for me because I am blind. When you grow up blind, the one thing everyone constantly teaches you is to never be afraid of asking for help.

Even so, I spent several years trying to do most all the work by myself.

When I started letting people help, my life changed. My website traffic grew, my Alexa ranking skyrocketed, and I began getting featured on many websites and podcasts.

Sometimes, I openly asked for help. Other times, people saw what I was trying to do and freely offered their time and abilities.

I'm going to tell you the secret that will help you with the whole idea of asking for help.

No, I don't mean if you ask, "What is the worst that can happen?" I'm not even going to claim that my favorite line is, "If you don't ask, they can't say 'Yes.'" It's neither of those.

The secret it this: *If you don't ask someone to help, you are depriving them of an opportunity.*

You are robbing them of the chance to help another human being. You are keeping them from the pure joy that comes from doing something for someone else.

By *not* asking for help, the person who has the knowledge or skills you need is actually missing a chance to use the information he or she has gathered.

How do you know they aren't just waiting and begging for someone to come to them and say, "You know everything there is to know about this subject—could you please help me?"

Once you change your thinking on this subject, then you can not only ask for help, but feel good about doing so!

Now that you know this secret, it's time for another exercise.

Exercise 5

I want you to go back to your piece of paper that's divided into the four sections. Under the section for *I need help with it*, I want you to think if there are any new items from the other sections that you can move to this category. If you were as reluctant to ask for help as I was, then I'm guessing you didn't put much in this section. If you can move a few things to this section, *then move them now*. If you want to create a whole new piece of sectioned paper, go for it; otherwise, simply cross off each item or even draw a circle around each item and draw an arrow pointing it to the section it should be moved to. Easy.

Then, take some time to start asking for help. Contact people, or schedule a few appointments.

Because I want to keep you focused, I also want you to pick the one thing on this list that speaks to you as having the most potential impact on your journey, then call or email that person and either ask for help or make arrangements to meet with them to do so.

In addition, I want you to email me again with the item you chose, who you asked, and how it went. You may not get the answers you were hoping for. You are just learning how to ask for help. You may get more than you hoped for. ***The point here is to ask one person on your list for help and to do it right away.***

Did you know that asking for help can lead to unexpected surprises? It can.

I had to ask people how to use Twitter. I often have to ask technical support departments at companies for help navigating their sites with a screen reader. Sometimes, like with Indiegogo, they will offer to do it for me. Sometimes I get instructions and pointers. Other times, I have to ask a friend or family member to do things for me. I once had to ask a lady to help me put my own merchandise on my website. In the process, she volunteered to create a new logo for my company!

I currently have four or five people who know the login information to my websites and are welcome to go into my sites or blogs to fix problems or improve conditions. I had to learn to have faith in others. I also had to learn how to relax some of the control over my business.

The key is to realize that no one, no matter how smart, no matter how determined, can do it all. So, please accept that you will need to ask for help and start doing it *today*.

I hope the fact that you are reading this means that you are ready to reach out to others and let them help you move forward on your path. I also hope you remember this time in your life, later, when *you* are the expert, and people start coming to *you* to ask for help and guidance. They will!

Stop reading now and complete this exercise. Once you have done that, come back, and continue reading.

MAXWELL IVEY JR.

Step 6: Staying Motivated by Taking Small Steps

One of the biggest problems people face when starting anything new is how to stay motivated.

There are going to be days when you just don't feel like getting out of bed or working on your new project. There are going to be days when life gets in the way, in the form of your regular job, spouse, children, entertainment, household chores, etcetera. So, how do you stay motivated?

Take many small steps, and never stop stepping!

Up to now, I have been pushing you to take action on one or two items as a way of getting you started. As we all know, starting is easier than continuing to follow the steps needed to accomplish your goal. There are undoubtedly many smaller goals on your list that must be accomplished before you can even be on the road towards that imagined goal. There will also be many obstacles to overcome. Some of them you will have anticipated, and others will be total surprises.

What I need to remind you of is that the only way to achieve a big, grand dream is to take small steps every hour, day, week, month, and year.

I am an Eagle Scout. I'm actually one of the few blind Eagles. I was the first one to achieve this rank in the Sam Houston Area Council that includes most of Southeastern Texas. It took me the better part of four years, but I didn't start out with the intention of being an Eagle Scout!

I was happy to be part of a group. At first, I was taught basic skills that led to skill awards. Then I progressed through the ranks of Tenderfoot, Second Class, and First Class. I was excited to go to summer camp where I earned merit badges. With more badges and some projects there were the ranks of Star, Life, and—finally—Eagle.

All along the way, my friends were pushing me to do more. We routinely had at least one ceremony a year called a Court of Honor where our achievements were recognized in front of our friends and families.

Your journey will be no different. It will involve taking many baby steps on the way to completion.

Another example of me taking many steps is my whole experience of having gastric surgery. I thought that having surgery meant no work. I found out that, like a lot of things in life, having the surgery was just a tool to help me on my way. I still had to change my diet, start taking vitamin supplements, and get more exercise.

I also had to lose at least 25 pounds prior to surgery. I went to classes where professionals helped me with this.

The best thing I learned is that I didn't have to change everything all at once.

The nutritionist said, "Change one thing and do it faithfully for a month."

Then she said, "At the end of the month, add another change."

I started with quitting caffeine.

Next, I swapped liquids like juice, milk, and soda for water and solids like cheese, yogurt, and cottage cheese. Then I changed the size of the portions I ate.

It took *eight months* for my insurance provider to approve the surgery.

I lost a total of 80 pounds before the procedure was even scheduled. I thought about not having it, but then I remembered where I had been before. I knew that, without the help of the surgery, I would probably be right back where I started. I went from 512 pounds down to 255 (with my shoes on). I am now at my ideal weight for my height of 6'4'' and solid build. I am having no trouble maintaining this weight. People, especially women, are now saying I am handsome, sexy, and even hot!

But… getting from Point A to Point B was a process that lasted over two years.

I had to take many small steps, and take them every day.

I am still learning new tricks. I am at a really good weight but I want to reshape my body. I am having to learn about using free weights. I am considering taking yoga or getting a rower. I continue to follow up with the surgeon and my other physicians to stay healthy.

Good health is a key to success in any endeavor. I wouldn't have the confidence to be writing this book if I hadn't lost the weight and got in better condition.

I hope you have the determination and perseverance to take continuous action every day. Don't stop stepping, either! Taking steps will keep you motivated. I know; I speak from experience.

To help you get started with your steps, I have another exercise for you to do.

Exercise 6

I want you to look at each and every item you've put on your list and determine which ones can be broken down into smaller components, or steps. I then want you to rewrite them, with the individual steps underneath each of the main ones you started with.

Once you have done that, *I then want you to categorize them as to how soon you will be able to move forward on them, and then get a new piece of paper (or two or three) and rearrange them so the ones you can do most easily are at the top with the ones that are more and more difficult below in order of difficulty.*

Then I want you to email me with at least one item you will do today, one for the next day, one for two days from now, one for a week from now, and one for a month from now.

I don't want you thinking farther in advance than that, but I won't be surprised if some of you do. If you plan too far in advance, you run the risk of overwhelming yourself with all you have to do before you start receiving the benefits of walking your path.

Stop reading now and complete this exercise. Once you have done that, come back, and continue reading.

MAXWELL IVEY JR.

Step 7: Celebrate Your Accomplishments

To stay motivated, you must celebrate every accomplishment.

As you continue to move down your path, towards your goal, you will have to find ways to stay motivated. This is because there are going to be some days when you just aren't going to feel like getting out of bed, much less like working on your additional activities. And there are going to be times your life will interrupt your plans.

It is natural and good for you to have a balanced life that includes family, hobbies, sports, entertainment, etcetera. I am not suggesting that anyone should be so focused that they don't have a life beyond their goals. The bottom line is this: How do you keep moving forward during those times when you don't have the energy to proceed?

I have a few ideas that will help here. The first thing is to celebrate every little accomplishment. You aren't always going to be successful. Sometimes, your ideas will not work. Sometimes, they may work too well. You may have to put off some of your plans until your skills or budget allow. However, when you do something right, it is important that you take the time to acknowledge it. Do *something* to recognize the accomplishment, whether it's taking time out to have a really good cup of coffee, read a book, watch a movie, or catch a sporting event or favorite show on TV.

You can do *something* for a while without having your laptop open or without being busy on your cell phone. You could go for a walk or get in a workout. You could post a Tweet or Facebook status update. You could write a blog post or record a video. You could even call or email someone with the news, although this one can be tricky because our friends don't always understand what it is we are doing or why.

You know what would make you happy, so pick something in relation to the size of the achievement and do that. You will find that celebrating becomes contagious. The more often you take time out to say, "Hey, I did good," the more things you will notice that you have managed to cross off of your list.

It's easy to stay motivated when you celebrate every accomplishment, because you will become addicted to success and will want to revel in your achievements! I mentioned coffee because a good cup of hazelnut cappuccino is like ambrosia to me.

I love listening to old-time radio shows, so sometimes I will listen to one I haven't heard yet without checking my email or answering the phone. I also love a great story, so having uninterrupted reading time is a good celebratory action for me, too.

Whenever I make a sale, my brother, Patrick, takes a picture of the check and saves it on his phone. He does that for me. I recently found a company that can turn photos into paintings. I plan to have photos of my latest sales converted to artwork for the office I hope to open someday.

Of course, the best is when I've made that sale and the money is in the bank so I can write a blog post about it and call all my family with the news.

Exercise 7

By now you should have done a few of the things you have identified as part of your overall plan.

Now, I want you to send me an email telling me what it was, how long it took, how you felt, and what you did to reward yourself. I can't view photos, but if you took some that you want to share, give yourself bonus points.

Stop reading now and complete this exercise. Once you have done that, come back, and continue reading.

MAXWELL IVEY JR.

Step 8: Find the Good in Everything and Be Positive

I know you have probably heard people speak about the power of a positive mindset. You might have even heard some mention that being an optimist or having a positive outlook has helped make them successful.

It's true. My experiences serve as a prime example of how staying positive has helped me accomplish the many things I have.

I'll tell you a secret about becoming a positive person and staying one: *it's not easy to be positive.*

You have to *choose* to be happy. You have to *look* for the signs that things are improving.

I can tell you, from experience, that there are going to be days where finding those rainbows or silver linings is a *struggle*. I am reminded of the movie Little Giants, which is about two rival Pop Warner football teams from a small town in Texas. The kids on the underdog team managed to get one yard on their first possession of the second half. The linesman changed the down and distance marker from *1st and 10* to *2nd and 9*. This, along with some Disney magic, turned them into heroes.

Sometimes it can be that simple, where all you need is to find one little thing, that one small bit of success, that you can hang your hat on.

I am also reminded of the time when I sold a big carousel for a man from Vermont. The ride sold in about two months, from first listing to closing. After the sale closed, the owner refused to return my emails, texts, and phone calls. He didn't pay me, either.

I have since realized that he isn't going to pay me, ever. I also found out, to my dismay, that I never received anything in writing saying he *would* pay me. That is my fault, I know, but the day I realized I neglected to have him sign a contract was a really hard one.

I could have blasted him on social media, but I thought that would do more harm than good. I could have moped around, and maybe even decided to quit, but I, instead, decided to make a list of the positives that came out of this experience. I felt good, knowing I could sell such an item so quickly. My faith in the strength of my social media networks was affirmed. I had mentioned the sale online and received a lot of positive comments. The Mutual of Omaha *Aha Moment* people saw it and rewarded me with a $100 Amazon gift card, which I used to buy my first new clothes since having my gastric bypass surgery. I got a lot of new traffic to my website and even acquired some new listings. I also got requests from people needing help finding a specific piece of equipment.

Even though I lost out on my payment, there was still a lot to be happy about.

I hope you will remember to look for the good things that are happening in your life (or your business) *every day*. The signs will be there, but you have to know they are there just waiting for you to notice them. Like I said, some days, it's hard work being happy, but if you focus on the positive, the negative won't seem so bad.

To further illustrate my points, I'm going to tell you about another of my experiences.

Before the writing of this book, I participated in an online summit, as a viewer. The fact that I'm blind did not deter me. In order to watch the videos, viewers had to enter a contest to win online coaching products. I entered, not thinking I would ever win, but by the middle of the second week, it looked like I would win. I went all-out in my promotion of the link that would make me one of the winners. On the final day, there was a technical problem caused by the fact that I use a screen reader. I thought there was a chance I wouldn't be able to claim the prize if I won it. Happily, this did not happen.

A friend contacted the summit organizer, on my behalf, in the proper method, and I was declared their third-place prize winner. But I had already decided to be happy with the victory. I mean, there I was, a blind blogger competing against hundreds of other online marketers (many of whom have much larger social media networks than I do), and I was going to at least finish in the top five, or even the top three!

I had decided that I would post the final leaderboard on my site and share the experience. I knew people would be inspired to hear the story, and they were. I was told by many of my readers that they were on the edge of their seats and that my win encouraged them to redouble their efforts.

So, don't just think positively, but act like a success. Knowing you are a success and telling yourself you are every so often is great; but nothing is better for the ego than to stand, walk, and talk like it.

To get you started, here are some of my thoughts regarding my contest experience. It didn't cost me any money to try. If I hadn't done it, and it had turned out well for someone else, how would I feel? I learned an important lesson. I didn't let anyone ruin my day or my experience. I stayed true to who I am as a person. I helped someone. I didn't focus on whether I was rewarded or not.

To help you find the good in your life, I've got another exercise for you to do.

Exercise 8

This one might be a little difficult for you than the other exercises, but it'll provide you with a way to help you change your mindset into a more positive one.

Think of a recent experience where you thought the worst happened. Write one sentence about it. Then make a list of all the good that came out of it. You may have to be creative to find a positive. Like celebrating accomplishments, this will get easier the more you do it.

Stop reading now and complete this exercise. Once you have done that, come back, and continue reading.

MAXWELL IVEY JR.

Step 9: Allow Positivity to Enter Your Life and Keep the Negativity Out

We have all heard that old saying about the best defense being a good offense. In my opinion, this applies perfectly with keeping the negativity out of your life. The more positive influences you have in your life, the better your chances are for success, in any endeavor.

How you build up your positive outlook starts with who and what you allow into your life.

Seek out positive, successful people, and surround yourself with them.

Remind yourself on a daily basis that you are choosing to be happy, positive, and successful.

Make healthier choices.

The more you seek out positive books, movies, TV shows, and friends, the better off you will be.

I read a lot. I have always read as part of my recreation, for enjoyment. Now, I read to improve myself, too. Part of this is because so many great authors insist that you have to read in order to be a successful writer. In addition, as a blogger and website owner, I have to write well.

Because there are so many good stories out there, I divide my reading into fiction, biographies, autobiographies, and personal development. I find my inspiration in authors from people like Joel Osteen, Steven Covey, Joyce Meyer, and Wayne Dyer to Tom Sullivan, Rachael Scdoris, Helen Keller, and Erik Weihenmayer.

When I began making changes to my reading habits, the biggest thing for me was deciding not to be a snob about what I read. For a long time, I avoided authors like Dr. Phil, Dr. Laura, Elizabeth Gilbert, etcetera. I was okay with reading inspiring books from blind authors, other people with disabilities, and sports stars, but I refused to read any of the "self-help" authors.

Finally, I was convinced to try a couple after reading reviews written by bloggers I trust. Now, I will read a book by anyone if I think they have something meaningful to share.

Sometimes you need inspiration and motivation, and other times you just need the distraction of a good story.

When it comes to television, consider what you are watching. Every show doesn't have to have a positive message, but you should at least be conscious of what you are taking in. If you are like me, there are many shows you watch on a weekly basis. Often the decision to watch isn't something you have really thought about. Our decisions can be influenced by which news programs we watch. It could be that we watch shows we don't care for because they come on before or after one we are waiting for and look forward to. It could be that we are watching because friends or family tell us we just have to.

I just want you to think about what you are watching.

One thing I strongly recommend is to limit how much news you watch. I'm not advocating for you to be uninformed; I just know that the goal of most news departments is to scare or enrage their audience. You don't need to take in a lot of this kind of negativity! Keep it out so you can concentrate on the positive! I limit myself to one hour of news a day. Given the amount of replay, there is very rarely a need to watch more.

Consider your use of technology, and how you use social media, too, when trying to allow positivity to enter your life.

How do you use the Internet? Do you spend hours reading posts on Facebook and Twitter?

Do you get wrapped up in the lives of your online friends or celebrities? Are you addicted to any of the social-media-based games?

This is another area where I think I am better off for being blind. Since I use a screen reader, accessing Facebook, LinkedIn, Twitter, etcetera, isn't as easy for me. So, my primary method for using social media sites is to only visit to post status updates or share my friends' content. After that, I only return if I get an email notification that requires me to log in to answer it.

I understand social sites are distracting, so do what you can to decrease the temptation.

The toughest problem we face when trying to keep the negativity out of our lives is that of negative people. This is one area where you really need to push to eliminate the negative.

One truly toxic person can totally drain you of the energy it takes to stay positive and move forward.

If it is a co-worker, then don't drink coffee, take smoke breaks, or eat lunch with that person. If it is a friend, then you need to find someone else to enjoy activities or attend events with. If it is a neighbor, then don't borrow things from him or her and don't plan to do things together. I know eliminating negativity from your life is not going to be easy, but it is *critical* to your success and future happiness.

You might be thinking that eliminating negative people from your life isn't always possible, and I'm going to agree with you. It's difficult to do when it comes to family members and roommates. I know; I share a house with my younger brother and I've had to walk away from him, go to another room, go hang out in the garage, put on my headphones, etcetera, just to keep a positive mindset.

If you can't eliminate from your life the people who are bringing you down, then you need to minimize the impact they have on your health and well-being.

Think about how you feel after spending time with a negative, the-world-is-coming-to-an-end type of person. I'm willing to bet that your outlook and your feelings are more negative, too.

Consider the influences of your online "friends" as well as people in your daily life. If you encounter people online who are bringing you down from 3,000 miles (or more) away, they are hurting your chances for improvement. No matter what you do, chances are you probably can't turn them into a happy person. You are welcome to try, but if they aren't willing to improve themselves, then they are probably just calling emailing, or hanging out with you in person to have someone to listen to them.

You have to protect yourself and preserve the stores of energy you have. You can't be wasting them on people who do nothing but drain your energy and dampen your spirits.

In addition to removing these negative people or lessening their impact, you should also be seeking out positive role models or mentors. You should look for people who are doing what you want and pattern yourself after them. You should also attempt to meet them in person or connect with them through social media.

Exercise 9

As a result of reading this section, you're probably considering a few changes you can make in your attempts to eliminate negativity from your life and allow positivity to enter it.

I want you to take a hard look at who and what you are allowing—and going to allow from now on—into your heart and mind, and what you're going to change.

Take a few moments to write them down, on a fresh piece of paper. Consider the books, movies, TV shows, music, and people that you are no longer going to allow to be a part of your life, and what you can do to minimize their negative effects.

When you feel your list is complete, put it into play. Take action. Make the changes. *Then let me know how things go. Email me; I want to know the changes you're making to allow positivity to enter your life and keep the negativity out of it. I'd also like to hear about something you have added based on my suggestions.* Is there a new mentor in your life? Have you decided to approach someone for this roll? Have you made an appointment or sent an email? Have you purchased any new books, or even browsed some on Amazon or in a book store? Did you encounter any problems? Did you find solutions on your own, or do you need some more advice?

If you email me with the details, I can help you further. Remember, I'm your friend, your coach, and your rock.

Stop reading now and begin this exercise. Once you have made your initial list, come back, and continue reading.

MAXWELL IVEY JR.

Step 10: Look at the Big Picture and Describe Your Success

Earlier, we talked about celebrating your small successes. Now we are going to look at your big goal and your overall definition of what success means to you.

It is important that you decide in advance what success means to you, because *being successful* means different things to different people.

What are the factors that you will use to measure your success? What does being a "winner" look like to you? Will you have to live like a rock star to be successful? Or will making enough of a living to support your family and spend more time with them provide you with satisfaction?

Do you need to be the absolute best in your field, or will being one of the more respected members of a profession be acceptable?

Does your definition even include financial rewards? Does it include freedom, or freedoms? What kind, or kinds?

One thing to remember when deciding on your definition is that it is important to separate professional or emotional success from financial victory.

You can be making big strides and accomplishing more and more every day but still not see financial rewards, or results in your bottom line.

I am constantly reminding myself of this difference. When it comes to selling amusement park and carnival rides, I am considered one of the experts. I am respected for being an ethical broker, but I am in a competitive market. Making sales doesn't happen as often or as easily as I would prefer, and sometimes the commissions don't come in for weeks after my part of making the sale has ended.

To cope with the delay in the financial reward, I remind myself how difficult the job is and take satisfaction in every sale. I especially love it when I win out over companies with more resources, who have been in the business much longer than I have been. I also love it when people contact me directly asking for my help to determine what equipment they should buy and then help them locate items suitable to their needs.

I have two different pictures of success; one for each of my business ventures.

For the Midway Marketplace, I have three goals, and when I attain them, I will feel like I've achieved my success with this business. My goals are as follows: (1) I want to get to the point of selling at least a million dollars' worth of equipment each year, with at least one new ride sold each year; (2) I want to generate at least $1000 of ad revenue each month; and (3) I want to travel to my clients' homes and start doing YouTube shows based on their equipment.

For my new business as a coach and speaker, I want to get my first paid speaking engagement by the end of January 2015. I want my first client-based testimonial. I have two testimonials already, but they are from friends, not clients. I would also like to receive at least three good reviews for this book. Notice that I didn't mention I wanted a ton of book sales; I want to reap rewards other than simply earning cash. I get satisfaction from helping others, and knowing I helped others. That is what success means to me with respect to my coaching business.

So, now I'll ask you again: What does success look like *to you*?

Exercise 10

Make a list of the possible ways you could feel successful in your new endeavor. Include recognition from professional associations, client and customer testimonials, personal satisfaction with a job well done, and, of course, financial rewards. Then tell me what your bottom line is. What do you need to see happen in the next month, quarter, year, and five years from now, to consider yourself a winner?

Stop reading now and complete this exercise. Once you have done that, come back, and continue reading.

Step 11: Assess Your Failures, Re-evaluate, and Repeat

I've talked about celebrating accomplishments, big and small, as well as the value of deciding to be positive; but what happens when one of your ideas doesn't work?

We've all been there. You start something new—a weight loss plan or a college course or something else—to improve your life and you fail at it.

What you might not realize is that failure is not such a bad thing as long as you take it the right way, and realize that it's a part of being successful.

We have all heard the bromides about failure leading to success, but the reason there are so many quotes about the benefits of having to overcome adversity is because every great person has had to.

I was the fat kid in junior high, high school, college, and at work. People now call me Skinny-

Minnie or Mini-Max. No one would think of calling me Maxwell House any more, like they used to when they thought I was as big as a house!

When I was growing up, teachers used to ask my younger brother, Michael, if he was related to Max because they had him the year before and he was one of their best students. Nowadays people ask me if I'm related to Michael, the talented airbrush artist and show painter!

Simply put, we have all failed at some point in our lives, and we will all continue to fail, but understanding that failure is simply part of success is what will help make you even more successful.

I believe in my heart that sharing these thoughts with you is important. I can imagine publishing this book and changing many lives. I can also picture making a good living from selling this book, coupled with my coaching services. But what if it doesn't happen that way? It would be a setback, and a painful one, but would it end my efforts?

NO, for several important reasons.

First, I am a good writer, in general.

Writing is one of those things I've always been good at. With respect to this book, I will submit it to a professional editor I know before publishing it, and ask my friends to help me promote it.

Second, I live my life through the methods I've shared with you in these ten steps, so I would feel bad if I never shared or tried to share them with more people who are in need of hearing them.

Finally, I also believe that making any effort has *value*.

Writing this book was scary, due to the many things I didn't know. However, as I progress on my own journey, I will learn about the process of creating and publishing a book. I'll also learn about marketing it to others. The fact that I will be challenged the whole way does, indeed, bring me out of my comfort zone, but if we all remained in our comfort zones, we'd never grow, change, or be successful.

I've written several blog posts about the obstacles I've faced, and I've shared my trepidation and insecurities with others, too. If you don't follow my coaching blog already, I'd like to urge you to become a subscriber. I'll continue to write about my experiences, and I'll continue to be completely forthright and honest while doing so.

With respect to this book, I don't think it will be a flop. I am actually wondering what I'm going to do and how I'm going to feel if it is a big success. That's also scary, but in an exciting way!

Of course, the thing I want most of all is to help YOU.

Throughout this book, I have set up exercises where you are invited—if not required!—to email me with your progress.

Because I am including email support in the cost of this book, I've had to consider the following questions: What if I don't price it high enough and get overwhelmed to the point that I can't help people as quickly and thoroughly as they expect, and I make them mad? What if the price I have in mind for coaching is too high to allow me to help most people or so low that I run myself ragged?

There are all kinds of failures. When you experience one, you need to re-evaluate. You need to take a hard look at what you planned to have happen, what actually did happen, and what parts of your plan can be corrected or improved.

You need to consider different factors, too, during your re-evaluation. Is it possible the failure was caused by an improper assumption, or just poor timing? Did you count on someone to perform who let you down? Was there an unexpected problem with some aspect of your website, blog, podcast, or other technology-based item?

Once you have determined *why* you failed, the next step is to figure out *if* you are ready to try again, or *when* you will be able to. You should try to get right back at it as soon as possible, but don't be pressured by friends, family, business partners, or yourself to try again before you are actually ready.

The goal is to turn failures into successes, to use your adversity to grow your success muscles.

One of my early failures with the ride selling business was gaining new listings. I generally only got them from friends and family in the carnival end of the industry. People wouldn't reply to my phone calls or emails. I figured it was just because I was new and also because my site was commission-based instead of being a free, classified site with advertising. I finally decided that I would have to give something away, but I didn't know what that could be.

When I realized that everyone wants more traffic, and traffic can come from links, I offered free text links on my site in exchange for an email subscription. That particular decision has led to a robust mailing list and many pages of links on the site.

I am continuing to work that method and I am looking at hiring someone to start contacting these people to verify and update their information, as this will also give someone a chance to ask the owners if they need further assistance.

An area where I still haven't found success is with advertising. I wanted—and still want—sponsors for the Midway Marketplace. The site has huge traffic and a great Alexa ranking, but no one seems to want to advertise on it. I contacted many people, but didn't yield great results. I had—and still have—some free banner ads on the site, as examples, and I also have a *Submit Ad* page with rates, but I was—and still am—constantly emailing potential advertisers. I finally realized that the main problems are that I am not a marketing expert and that I needed help crafting a better pitch letter. I started reading articles on this subject, and began working with a coach of my own so that I could write better emails. This is a continuing process, but each failure gets me closer to success. If I keep pounding on the door or keep improving the tool I am hitting the door with, I know that, eventually, I will knock it down. I hope this inspires you to keep banging away.

Exercise 11

I want you to share with me an instance where you failed. Take a long, hard look at what happened and why, then tell me what you learned from the experience and how you would turn that failure into a success now.

I would especially love to hear about that instance if it is something that has happened since you started reading this book.

MAXWELL IVEY JR.

Temporary Parting Words

I wish I could tell you that you will get to a point where there is no more work, but I just can't do that. In the first place, things change, and so do people. You aren't the same person you were a few minutes, hours, or days ago. Things that used to work in the beginning may no longer work for you. There will be new tools available for you to use. The Internet, blogging, podcasting, social media, etcetera, are constantly evolving, and you may find yourself no longer satisfied with what you are doing or how you are doing it.

Therefore, you need to regularly take stock of where you are, what you are doing, and where you are going.

It may be that you come to believe there is something bigger for you than the goal you originally set for yourself. It could be that you discover there is more inside you than you thought there was, or that there even could be.

That has happened to me. I had no idea my work online was inspiring people. I didn't plan to become a coach or motivational speaker. I didn't even plan to be a spokesperson or representative of the blind and visually impaired community.

Yet, here I am, offering coaching services and seeking forums to share my message of using a positive attitude and consistent hard work to accomplish your goals and reach your dreams.

I am also now a peer advisor for the American Foundation for the Blind, and am helping other blind people.

Writing this book was never on my radar. You will be the judge of how good a job I have done, but I feel like a success *already*, for having written it.

Most importantly, I've learned that I get a lot of joy from helping others, and I can't wait to find out what it feels like to give a speech and help dozens—if not hundreds—of people at one time.

I am looking forward to sharing my success stories from my clients in blog posts, too.

While selling amusement equipment has been my focus for over eight years now, I'm also looking forward to being able to delegate more of the duties to others so I can help more people as a coach and mentor.

What are your dreams? Share them with me. Let's work together to make them a reality. Choose a coaching package today, and find out how we can meet and speak. I want you to become a success!

Throughout this book, I've kept my promise to be honest with you, and I have. Before I go, I want to thank you from the bottom of my heart. I know you chose me from a pond of options. I also know that turning over your hard-earned money is never easy, even though the amount isn't as important as the faith it takes to spend it.

You have put your trust in me, hoping that I have learned something that I can share with you in a way that you haven't heard before, and you are believing that—having done this—you will finally make that quantum leap forward in your life.

I appreciate your investment of time, money, faith and trust, and I want to thank you.

You have my word that I will continue to do my best to help you walk your path and to be a success as you travel on your journey from the darkness into the light.

MAXWELL IVEY JR.

About the Author

Born into a family of carnival owners in Texas, USA, Maxwell Ivey lost his sight at age 12. Having a natural gusto for life, Max graduated college and became heavily involved in the Eagle Scouts.

He also worked in the family business alongside his brothers until his father succumbed to lung cancer.

Faced with his own mortality, Max made some life-altering changes.

He underwent gastric surgery and lost over 250 pounds. He started his own business, buying and selling amusement rides, and learned how to blog using software for visually-impaired people.

Overcoming many obstacles, Max made a name for himself online and now shares his experiences on The Blind Blogger.

Max's favourite things entail teaching and helping others achieve their goals and so he began another business: personal coaching.

Max now spends his days singing, reading, blogging, working, writing, creating videos, and coaching.

Max would like to travel the world one day and meet his many online friends and clients in person. He'd also like to meet a special lady to share his life with!

Maxwell Ivey can be found on social media, too, so please connect with him on:

1: Facebook at
https://www.facebook.com/Mr.Midway

2: LinkedIn at
https://www.linkedin.com/in/maxwellivey

3: Twitter using @maxwellivey or
https://twitter.com/maxwellivey

4: The Midway Marketplace at
http://midwaymarketplace.com/

To stay updated and be notified when other books are released, please visit The Blind Blogger at http://theblindblogger.net/ and sign up to Max's email list!

About *It's Not the Cookie, It's the Bag: An Easy-to-Follow Guide for Weight Loss Success*

Everyone knows that changing your lifestyle is not easy. Whether you are trying to lose weight or trying to keep it off, you need an action plan you can follow. The thing is... it doesn't have to be hard. It can be fun, simple, and easy!

In It's Not the Cookie, It's the Bag, blind man Maxwell Ivey Jr shares the ups and downs of his weight loss—and weight maintenance—journey to good health.

He also reveals the exact methods he uses in his day-to-day life to achieve and maintain his phenomenal success.

Going from 512 pounds to a 250-pound, lean, mean machine in just two years, Max tells you how YOU can replicate his success and become the person you want to be... the person you were meant to be... the person you deserve to be... one small step at a time.

So what are you waiting for?

Get started today!

Use Max's methods to become happy for the rest of your life!

After all, if a blind man can do this, why can't you?

If you purchase this book from Selz via https://maxwellivey.selz.com/, it will enable Max to earn a higher royalty percentage.

You can also purchase it in e-book or print format from Amazon.

About *The Blind Blogger's NYC Adventures (+ How You Can Make YOUR Dreams Come True)*

This is the true story of Maxwell Ivey and his adventures in New York City. It contains many life lessons and explains how you can make your dreams come true, using the keys to success Max regularly uses to attain his own goals and make his dreams a reality.

Max is a blind entrepreneur, blogger, author, and podcaster. He won Amtrak's 2016 prestigious Writers in Residency Award, which included a trip to any city in the USA. He chose to travel to NYC... alone! He chronicled each of his adventures, which include being on a TV show, going ice-skating in Rockefeller Center, meeting the Blogger from Paradise in person... and more!

Max displays a remarkable amount of courage and willingness to chase his dreams, despite the obstacles in his way. He is a great role model who teaches others how they can work towards their dreams and ultimately reach them... no matter what.

Using creative narration, accompanying photos, and funny stories, Max also makes the readers laugh with his witticisms about being blind... as in the case of sitting backwards on the train, because the scenery is the same regardless of which way he is facing.

This is Max's first book in his travel series.

Read it. Enjoy it. Learn from it. And become armed with the secrets to achieving your own dreams, too!

If you purchase this book from Selz via https://maxwellivey.selz.com/, it will enable Max to earn a higher royalty percentage. You can also purchase it in e-book or print format from Amazon.

Max has since travelled to other places, and is working on more books! To stay updated and be notified when other books in this series are released, please visit The Blind Blogger at http://theblindblogger.net and sign up to Max's email list!

About The Blind Blogger's First Speaking and Signing Adventures (+ How You Can Conquer Your Fears)

Close your eyes and imagine yourself taking a trip alone, on a tiny budget. Now, imagine taking that same trip without having sight.

Meet Max—a fearless, witty, inspiring individual who thinks nothing of traveling across the country by himself. On a limited budget, while missing trains, dealing with luggage and mobility issues, and facing unexpected circumstances, Max was determined to promote his books and become a motivational speaker.

In this second book in his travel series, Max shares wisdom gleaned from facing obstacles, teaches valuable lessons, and entertains you with stunning storytelling. Using humor and honesty, he bears his soul about the ups and downs of facing and overcoming fears and finding the positive in every situation. Commiserate with him when no one showed up at the bookstore, applaud his courage as he took the microphone and gave a powerful speech, and laugh along with him as he cracks jokes about things being so easy that even a blind guy can do them!

This book is original, entertaining, helpful, and reassuring. It's also an incredible example of bravery as well as of someone who practices what he preaches and finds solutions instead of making excuses. Use Max's advice as you challenge yourself to chase your dreams, reach your goals, face your fears, and attain new levels of success.

Above all, enjoy the ride!

If you purchase this book from Selz via https://maxwellivey.selz.com/, it will enable Max to earn a higher royalty percentage. You can also purchase it in e-book or print format from Amazon.

This is the second book in Max's travel series. Max has since travelled to other places, and is working on more books! To stay updated and be notified when other books in this series are released, please visit The Blind Blogger at http://theblindblogger.net and sign up to Max's email list!

Made in the USA
Middletown, DE
20 November 2025

Made in the USA
Middletown, DE
20 November 2025